WADE'S
STORY

MARTIN L. ALTMAN III, "WOODIE"

G000075569

ISBN 978-1-0980-2556-4 (paperback)
ISBN 978-1-0980-3255-5 (hardcover)
ISBN 978-1-0980-2557-1 (digital)

Copyright © 2020 by Martin L. Altman III, "Woodie"

All rights reserved. No part of this publication may be reproduced, distributed, or transmitted in any form or by any means, including photocopying, recording, or other electronic or mechanical methods without the prior written permission of the publisher. For permission requests, solicit the publisher via the address below.

Christian Faith Publishing, Inc.
832 Park Avenue
Meadville, PA 16335
www.christianfaithpublishing.com

Printed in the United States of America

A true story of a brave young man and
his struggle with a deadly disease; the
faith in GOD that sustained him; the love
and support from his family, church, and
community; and the power of prayer.

The Anchor Holds

"This is my beloved SON, in whom I am well pleased."
—Matthew 3:17

My son is Wade Altman, whom I am very
proud of and love very much.
—Martin L. Altman III, "Woodie"

ACKNOWLEDGEMENTS

I am not sure how to begin the foreword to *Wade's Story*, so let me start by thanking everyone.

First of all, I would like to express my appreciation to the publishing company, hopefully there will be one.

Next, I am reminded of my pastor when he is thanking or recognizing those who have helped in the church or done work on a project. It is hard to remember everyone and not leave anyone out.

In sharing *Wade's Story*, there have been so many who have influenced his life. Coming to mind are the healthcare providers at Duke University Hospital, especially those in the Pediatric Bone Marrow Transplant Unit. All of them provided excellent care for Wade during his time there, and also for our daughter Blakely. As you will read, in my opinion the staff and facilities are some of the best in the world.

My wife Lisa and I made friends in Durham while we were there whom we may never visit or talk to again. Hopefully they will see this writing of *Wade's Story* and remember our time with them.

In writing and sharing *Wade's Story* I used social media and email. I received many encouraging comments and return emails from the followers of his story, saying how much they enjoyed the posts and notes and encouraging me to put them in book form.

Wade was born with a gift for singing and playing music, but many in his life helped him along that path and taught him how to improve his vocal skills and his musicality. Joey Carter, a local vocalist and musician, coached Wade for several years. Our music ministers at Maryville Pentecostal Holiness Church, Tommy and Kim Gordon, helped with praise and worship songs. Olivia Powell Huggins and Georgetown County Project Beach influenced Wade and improved his abilities all the more. Pastor Phillip McCart and the youth band at Screven Baptist Church, I thank them for bringing Wade into their group and for their mentorship.

Georgetown High School NJROTC taught Wade discipline and patriotism, and strengthened his body and mind. His Captain and Master Chief schooled him in respect and love for the military and his country.

Of course I must remember his teachers at Maryville Elementary and Georgetown Middle and High Schools, most of whom he loved and respected.

I certainly can't overlook all of his church family at Maryville, many of them his Sunday school teachers, and his pastors; Tommy and Ms. Ginny Cox, and David and Ms. Jho Coker.

As far as his immediate family and relatives in Georgetown and in the area, what an outpouring of love and support. During this time of Wade's life we were blessed to have so many close by.

Most of all I must thank God the Father, God the Son, and God the Holy Spirit for His grace, faithfulness, mercy, and direction in writing *Wade's Story* and for His love and miracles.

Wade is with Blakely and our friend Mary's golden retriever

Wade and Blakely, turtlenecks and tennis shoes

FAMILY NIGHT

Wade Hampton Altman was born September 18, 1986. We named him after his great-uncle Wade Hampton Barrineau, Jr., and his great-grandfather Wade Hampton Barrineau, Sr. My mother, Pearl Barrineau Altman, was of course thrilled with our choice of name for her youngest grandson. You will remember from South Carolina history that Wade Hampton I, II, and III are all heroes of the American Revolution, the War of 1812, and the Civil War, all in that order.

A green-eyed, blonde-haired, handsome boy full of life and mischief, Wade was never sick. He had never even thrown up.

In May of 1996, we went out on a family night to do some shopping and have dinner. Wade, Blakely, Lisa, and I stopped in a few stores before we went to the restaurant. We were enjoying supper when Wade said, "Mom, Dad, something weird happened. I was in the bathroom at the store looking in the mirror, and the next thing I knew, I woke up on the floor."

Our lives would never be the same.

Baby Wade, Woodie and Uncle Luckey
Merry Christmas 1986

REFERRALS AND REFERRALS

I will fear no evil, for YOU are with me.
—Psalm 23:4

We weren't sure what this was. Wade was fine, with not a mark on him. Blakely even teased and aggravated him like sisters do to brothers. Lisa decided to take Wade to the doctor the following Monday, just to make sure he was okay.

The doctor in Georgetown was a longtime family physician, delivering Blakely and Wade and even Lisa and her sisters. He also just wanted to make sure Wade was all right by doing lab work, as his examination showed no problems. Returning with results from the blood work, the usual look of calm and assurance on the doctor's face had turned to one of concern. Wade's blood work was abnormal. He would refer us to the local oncologist to review the lab findings. Lisa did not panic after this report, her faith sustaining her.

We waited to hear from the oncologist's office to schedule an appointment for Wade. Later there was a message at my office: the oncologist was trying to reach us. I returned the call right away and was immediately connected to the doctor. She said she would be referring us to MUSC, and that we should go as quickly as possible.

It was like a sucker punch to the gut! I could not breathe.

Cousin Kelci, Wade, and Blakely

AT MUSC

Surely goodness and mercy shall follow us all the days of our lives, and we will dwell in the house of the LORD forever.
—Psalm 23:6

The local oncologist made it clear, Wade should go to MUSC as soon as possible.

In the meantime, our son was as busy in life as ever. School was not his favorite time, but he made good grades, never cracking a book at home. His bedroom resembled a studio; recording and mixing equipment, guitars, amplifiers, keyboard, microphones and music stands, cords running everywhere. He once recorded a four-part harmony using only his voice with a track.

So that he would come out of the bedroom, Lisa kept the video games and his television in the corner of the family room. He could spend hours at this by himself or with a buddy, which would make them "testy," to say the least.

Warm weather was coming and there were no bigger beach bums on Pawleys Island than Wade, Blakely, and their cousin Kelci. On the ball field he played Dixie Youth; his first hit was a one bounce triple to left center. In his formation at martial arts class, Wade was stung by a wasp. He didn't move a muscle. We had no idea of the danger he was in.

Our appointment at MUSC was in the Pediatric Hematology and Oncology Wing in the Hollings Cancer Center. The doctor had studied Wade's records and had done the research. After the examination he was ready to make a diagnosis.

Video Gaming—Wade and Me

THE DIAGNOSIS

I will instruct you and teach you in the way you should go; I will counsel you with my eye upon you.
—Psalm 32:8

The oncologist/hematologist seemed eager to make his diagnosis, which was one we had never heard of: fanconi's anemia. Notice I did not capitalize the name, I refuse to.

At first we were glad the diagnosis was not cancer, but the more we learned about this disease the more concerned we became.

Swiss pediatrician Guido Fanconi had done extensive research on this blood disorder, thus the name. An inherited genetic anemia that leads to bone marrow failure, fanconi's anemia patients are usually aged twelve and younger with a variety of physical defects and low counts of white cells, red cells, and platelets. It is primarily a recessive disorder. If both parents carry the mutated gene, the children born have a 25 percent chance of developing fanconi's anemia. It is complicated, confusing, and sickening, but hold on! I mentioned miracles earlier and I will not let you down.

In 1996, the only treatment for fanconi's anemia was a bone marrow transplant, without which the future did not look good. The doctor at MUSC advised we do this as soon as possible, but there was a large problem. Wade would be his first patient for this procedure. We were not comfortable with this at all. Lisa almost immediately began searching for a second opinion.

As much as possible, we shielded Wade from all of this. I remember of only one time that he said he was afraid; I stayed in his room with him most of that night.

MIRACLES BEFORE WE KNEW

Lisa, Wade and Blakely

*Trust in the Lord with all your heart, and
lean not on your own understanding.*
—Proverbs 3:5

On February 2, 1985, Blakely Renee Altman was born. A normal childbirth with no complications, a miracle in itself. Meemaw, Blakely's grandmother, said, "Look what the GOOD LAWD has blessed ya'll wid!" The greater miracle here is that although Blakely had a one in four chance of being born with fanconi's anemia, she was and all of her life has been "as healthy as a horse." She has her own son now, Mason "Mase" Altman, born September 2, 2014, the picture of health and "wild as a buck."

You will remember Wade's birth date from earlier in his story. Also that children who are born with fanconi's anemia usually have many problems: thumb and arm deformities; skeletal defects of the hips, spine, or ribs; kidney problems; skin discoloration; gastrointestinal difficulties; and heart defects. Not Wade Altman, thank GOD! As I said, his first ten years, full of life and mischief.

When Wade was a baby, Lisa took him to the doctor with fever and congestion. His blood work was abnormal then, but was thought to have been caused by a virus. With his platelets being so low, he could have bled to death from any injury. We had no idea! Thus the third miracle in this writing; through all the bumps, bruises, cuts, scrapes, and falls that Wade endured growing up, there was never a problem with dangerous bleeding. A Covenant of Protection on his life.

In Lisa's search for a second opinion, she was able to contact Duke University Hospital in Durham, NC. They wanted to see Wade as soon as we could get him there.

DUKE UNIVERSITY
MEDICAL CENTER

Wade and Blakely in denim overalls and jeans

The prayer of a righteous man is powerful and effective.
—James 5:16

W e were all anxious and hopeful about going to Duke; it would be new for us. Wade and Blakely were glad to miss a day or two of school. Of course, after learning about Wade's condition we had to restrict his activity. Would he complain? Not a bit! He just spent more time with his books, video games, and music.

The trip to Duke University would be the first of many, SC Hwy 41, US Hwy 501, Interstate 95, and Interstate 40 becoming familiar territory.

The campus of Duke University and Medical Center is a beautiful place. Brownstone architecture is in or on every building. The gardens and landscaping are lush. There were doctors, nurses, students, and faculty all scurrying about carrying books and actually talking to each other. Very few cell phones if any to be seen. We were met by Carl, a family counselor of Child and Adolescent Life. He said he would be like our concierge during visits. A very friendly man, he took us on a short tour of the Medical Center. I noticed a man and woman coming from the children's wing who were crying. Carl saw them also and quickly moved to turn our attention.

We had lunch in the cafeteria with one of the administrators. I remember he had fruit and yogurt while we loaded up on pizza. He didn't seem pleased by our choice. Sorry! There was a funny moment that we can still laugh about today. After lunch we were in the long hallway outside of the cafeteria and noticed a young lady coming toward us. She was dressed in a business suit and very high heels walking fast. Close by us she slipped on one of those heels and almost went down. It was like an ice skater going to one hand and losing points. She popped up and kept going like she had not missed a step. When Blakely wears heels, she will always show us the move.

We spent the night in Durham to meet with the doctors the next day. There was a team of them ready to see Wade.

GOOD NEWS AND NOT SO GOOD NEWS

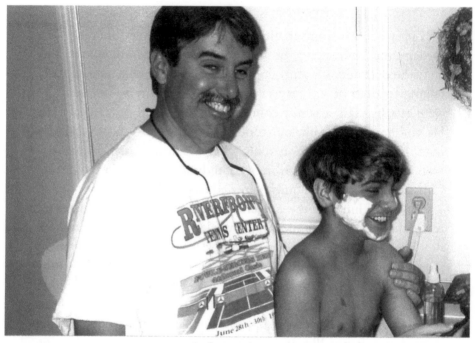

A shaving lesson

And we know that all things work together for them that love GOD, to them that are called according to HIS purpose.
—Romans 8:28

The following morning we visited with Wade's team of doctors. They took only a short time to examine him while we waited, his records having been studied. They provided a lot of information for us and it all was difficult to process in one meeting. Wade's diagnosis of fanconi's anemia did not change.

The good news was that the team agreed on Wade *not* immediately needing the bone marrow transplant (BMT). He would begin a series of bone marrow biopsies and aspirations so that his blood cell reproduction could be monitored closely. Thus we would begin regular trips to Duke Medical.

The not-so-good news was that the BMT would be inevitable. The doctors were confident that Wade's bone marrow would fail without the transplant, leading to spontaneous bleeding. We also learned the survival rate after the BMT would only be 60 percent and that matched bone marrow donors were usually very difficult to locate. It is now the fall of the year in 1996.

I am sure by now readers are wondering and asking why illness and tragedy and other things happen. Well, I can tell you this, we won't know why until that season and time comes. Nevertheless, there will be no testimony if there is no test! Thank you, Pastor Tommy Cox. I can also say this: first of all, Lisa and I did not have time to ask why or wonder why. We had to seek GOD for Wade's complete and total healing and to pray for HIS divine guidance in the days and weeks to come. Secondly, we had to make sure, without any doubt, that we would take Wade where he would receive the best care possible.

Take heart! Another miracle will be coming soon.

WHAT WERE THE CHANCES? ASTRONOMICALLY AGAINST!

On the evening of that day, the first day of the week, the doors being shut where the disciples were, for fear of the Jews, JESUS came and stood among them and said to them, "Peace be with you."
—John 20:19

Nana Pearl and Baby Wade

Before we could turn around (it seemed like anyway), we were back at Duke Medical Center. The need to begin searching for a bone marrow donor was urgent. The team explained the difficulty in finding a suitable donor and that a perfect matched donor, which would be the best for Wade, is nearly an impossibility. Even though the BMT was not immediately required, we needed to have the donor in place.

Biological parents as donors are not considered because of the gene that causes the problem. Siblings are next in line, then relatives, then an online search is started. I don't think I have to say what happens to a patient needing a donor when one is not found.

We learned that blood work is needed to determine the donor compatibility and that when the marrow is actually "harvested," as referred to, it is not a pleasant experience for the donor. Our daughter, Blakely, knowing all of this now, immediately stepped up to the plate! She did not hesitate! She jumped at the chance to help her brother. And Wade just turned ten years of age, living his life as any other ten-year-old would, only he has a rare and deadly disease. Does he cry, complain, or moan and groan? No! He walks with his head held high! He knows from where his healing and strength will come.

The team seemed almost reluctant to test Blakely for donorship, no confidence at all that she would be compatible and not wanting to put her through the needle and IV sticks. They even worried about her distress if she could not help Wade. Well… I won't make you wait until the next chapter. We witnessed THE HAND OF GOD MOVE! Blakely was a perfect match! The doctors were amazed! Most of them thanked GOD right along with us. This was a miracle for Wade and our family.

BONE MARROW BIOPSIES AND ASPIRATIONS BEGIN

Baby Wade and Cousin Kip

Do not let your heart be troubled; believe in GOD, believe also in ME. In my FATHER'S house are many dwelling places; if it were not so I would have told you; for I go to prepare a place for you.
—John 14:1–2

Lisa and I were marveling at the works of the LORD and HIS answers to prayer. We were thankful and relieved that Blakely was a perfect match bone marrow donor for Wade and for her eagerness to help her brother. We were all continuing to pray that Wade would not require the transplant.

Near the end of 1996 we returned to Duke and began Wade's bone marrow testing. The biopsies and aspirations would give the doctors a better understanding of the number of new blood cells developing and how healthy they were. Wade was under general anesthesia during the procedure. A needle large enough to withdraw a specimen of bone marrow and soft tissue was inserted into his hip. Lasting about thirty minutes, it seemed like an eternity.

Other than being groggy for a few minutes, Wade came through the procedure with no problems. Soon he was bouncing around as usual with no complaints, lots of different things to keep him busy in the children's waiting area. The doctor's report on the testing was again good and bad. They confirmed the transplant was not critical at that time, but his condition had regressed.

After our first trip to Duke, I visited with Pastor David Coker and his wife, Ms. Jho, of our church, Maryville Pentecostal Holiness. We talked about all that had been going on with Wade. They were very understanding and encouraging, even sharing stories I had not heard about. It seems that Wade had a habit of slipping into the fellowship hall and helping himself to ice cream. Pastor Coker soon tired of chasing Wade out of the hall and reprimanding him, this happening on weekdays. He decided, if he could not beat him, to join him, as the old saying goes. Wade and Pastor Coker began sharing ice cream in the fellowship hall and from there a special friendship grew!

Without Internet or cell phone, Pastor Coker started the Wade Altman Fund. We had no idea until the desperately needed monetary gifts began arriving. Support coming from our family, church, relatives, friends, and people in the community. This was such a blessing!

The bone marrow testing was scheduled every other month. We had to continue closely monitoring Wade's activity.

THE GEORGETOWN REVIVAL

My Bunch at Aunt Linda's on Sullivan's Island,
Thanksgiving 2015

HE will lead you to conquer in trials.
—Romans 8:37

The winter and spring months of 1997 were good for us. Continuing to monitor Wade's activity closely, we tried to make sure he could not get injured. This became difficult because of his new love for skateboarding. His vocal and musical skills steadily improved, along with the video gaming and skateboard prowess. These talents and hobbies would be a blessing in the future, not only for Wade but for all of us. Although the ongoing bone marrow testing indicated no improvement and only regression, his spirit had been touched and his faith was growing.

Many people were blessed, encouraged, and healed during the Georgetown Revival that went on for several months. I am struggling to describe Wade's experience at the altar, no doubt THE LORD was covering him in a mighty way. His chest was heaving and the veins in his neck and forehead were protruding and the look on his face was one of joy and bliss! There was no question that Wade had been delivered. He was happier, stronger, and at peace with whatever the future held. Yes, he is only ten years old and still doing what ten-year-old boys do, but complaints—NONE.

I would like to thank Evangelist Marvlene Branch and the musicians, singers, altar workers, prayer team, and everyone else who had a part in the Georgetown Revival. I now know the amount of time, effort, work, and prayer that is required in these ministries.

MAKE A WISH

Our family with Make-A-Wish at Disneyworld

*Consider it all joy my brethren, when you
encounter various trials, knowing that the
testing of your faith produces endurance.*
—James 1:2–3

My niece Marti did all of the work in connecting us with Make-A-Wish. The only thing left was for Wade to decide on his wish, and he chose Disneyworld. Thank you so much, Marti.

They flew us all down to Orlando, had a new rental car waiting, and lodged us at "Give Kids the World Village" just out of town. We were all treated so nice by everyone involved. Make-A-Wish is a wonderful organization, I can't say enough good about them. Not only did each of us have a pass to every attraction, we were always directed to the front of the line, no waiting at all. "Give Kids the World" was a great little place to stay. All of our meals were provided as well as personal time with the Disney characters. After visiting with other families there, we counted our blessings.

In the softball season of 1997, Blakely's talent blossomed. We followed her with the Georgetown County All-Stars to several tournaments, her team eventually falling short of the South Carolina title. Blakely is at least the third generation Altman ballplayer in Georgetown. Her great grandfather probably played as well, but I have not researched. I do know that he was a policeman in town. Wade gladly tagged along with skateboard in hand, exploring the concrete and asphalt around the ballparks.

Nearing the end of 1997 Wade's condition continued to regress. His bruising and discoloration were prevalent, nose bleeds started and became more often. His team at Duke believed it was time for the transplant, his latest bone marrow test results were not good.

This is what Lisa and I were faced with: the doctors said without the transplant Wade would not recover. If we went forward with it there was only a 60 percent chance he would survive the transplant. We had to seek GOD for His wisdom and guidance before we could make a decision.

WE MUST DECIDE

Wade is at Nana Pearl's enjoying cake under her table

I will say of the LORD, HE is my refuge and my fortress, my GOD, in whom I trust.
—Psalm 91:2

After much prayer and consultation we believed the BMT was the best option for Wade. Even though the chance of his surviving the transplant remained at only 60 percent, the alternative according to the doctors would be unthinkable.

The time was near Christmas of 1997, and we began making preparations for his transplant. In no way, shape, or form did this decision affect our faith for Wade's healing. We continued to pray and believe.

Wade's Aunts Kay, Linda, Byrtie, and their families joined us for lunch at the Orange Blossom Café a few days before Christmas. Not only did they bless us monetarily, but also with the latest PlayStation equipment for Wade. He was thrilled, and we were thankful.

The team at Duke advised us to get ready for a long stay, possibly all of 1998. They helped enroll Wade in homebound school during his hospitalization and recovery. Blakely's Aunt Kay and Uncle Luckey along with her Meemaw Argerine and Big Pop George would take care of her while we were at Duke. Other than a few days while her bone marrow was harvested, she would not miss school or JV softball. Once again we were thankful. Everyone was pulling together for us. For our lodging we located an RV park close to the hospital. Wade's Uncle Terry let us use his travel trailer as long as we needed it. In January of 1998 on a cold rainy day, after working the night before at International Paper, George along with Argerine pulled the RV from Georgetown to Durham and set it up. Our appreciation could not be expressed in words.

During the last week of January we settled in the camper. The day before Wade was admitted to the hospital we had a day of fun. Lisa and Blakely went shopping while Wade and I went to see *Titanic*. The next morning we checked Wade into the Pediatric Bone Marrow Transplant Unit in Duke University Hospital. Meemaw and Big Pop took Blakely back to Georgetown. These were tough days for Lisa and me.

DUKE UNIVERSITY PEDIATRIC BONE MARROW TRANSPLANT UNIT

Woodie and sisters Kay, Linda and Byrtie

GOD will supply all your needs according to
His riches in glory in CHRIST JESUS.
—Philippians 4:19

W e had visited the children's hospital and clinics many times in the past eighteen months, but this was our first day inside the PBMTU. The first set of doors opened into a large entranceway where there was a hand-washing station. Detailed instructions were posted about the importance of thorough hand-washing before entering the Unit. Also clearly posted were statements indicating visitors with any infection, internal or external, were not to enter the Unit.

The second set of doors opened into the first hallway. Children of all ages and nationalities were being treated in the Unit. Some had recovered enough to be in the hallway pushing around their IV poles and pumps. Others not as fortunate yet were in their rooms. All were accompanied by a loved one and had on filter masks. The Unit was in the shape of a horseshoe with the family room and kitchen in the center hall. Wade's room was the next to the last on the right.

The entranceway, each hallway, the family room, kitchen, and each child's room were equipped with a HEPA air filtration system. Wade's room was large and comfortable. He was especially excited about the latest model television and was looking forward to installing his new PlayStation.

Any infection is life-threatening to these children, thus all the precautions that were taken. No expense was spared, and I am sure other safety measures we were not aware of.

FINANCIAL MIRACLES

Healthsource®

A CIGNA HealthCare Company

February 16, 1998

Dr Denise Adams , Assistant Professor of Pediatrics
Pediatric Hematology-Oncology
Duke University Medical Center
228 Baker House
Durham, N.C. 27710

Re: Wade Altman   HS# 250988676*04

Dear Dr Adams:

This letter is to inform you that the matched related allogenic bone marrow transplant for the above member has been approved at Duke University Medical Center. The pre-certification authorization for this procedure is 104829.

Please see the enclosed information sheet that was sent to Jackie McPherson, Transplant Coordinator at Duke.

Please feel free to contact me if you have any questions or need additional information regarding this member & this authorization.

Sincerely,

Barbara Jackson, RN

Case Manager

Healthsource SC

CC: member

HEALTHSOURCE SOUTH CAROLINA, INC.
146 FAIRCHILD STREET   CHARLESTON, SOUTH CAROLINA 29492-9901   803-884-4063   800-962-8811

Healthsource approval letter

Those who know YOUR name trust YOU, for YOU,
LORD, have never forsaken those who seek YOU.
—Psalm 9:10

My wife, Lisa, has been in the background sometimes during this story, but she has not been idle. On the contrary, she has put in great time and effort securing the best care available for Wade. You will remember after his diagnosis of fanconi's anemia, and I continue refusing to capitalize, she immediately went to work on the telephone and writing letters for a second opinion and for the best care available. She was able to make an appointment with Duke University Hospital and we were comfortable and confident with their response. The only problem was with our health insurance.

Our insurer at that time was a South Carolina-based HMO group policy with my work. Because we were seeking treatment for Wade in North Carolina, the company initially did not approve coverage for his care. Well… I am here to tell you my wife would have none of that! She went to work right away with US mail and telephone in hand, going all the way up this insurance companies ladder! After weeks of this struggle we received the letter copy approving Wade's care at Duke. Another miracle from GOD and a valiant effort from Lisa.

During this time in Wade's story I was working with Liberty Life Insurance Company. Regional Vice President Tom Propes was my trainer, mentor, supervisor, and now my friend. Of course I was concerned about my income and my job in the future. As I said earlier, Wade's treatment and recovery could last up to one year, during which time Lisa and I would have to be in Durham. Before I had a chance to write Tom, he visited me! He said not to worry about a thing. When I could come back to work my job would be there and my income would continue while we were at Duke. He said I had accumulated a large amount of sick leave and could access the benefits while I had to be away! I had no idea. This was more than I could ask for.

Praise the Lord; thank You, Jesus! With these two miracles and with the Wade Altman Fund we did not have to worry about finances. We could then concentrate on Wade's treatment and care.

Wade's first invasive treatment was scheduled for Tuesday, February 17, 1998. This was surgical insertion of the central venous line catheter. He was not worried at all because he knew the Hickman would replace all the needle sticks. Lisa and I and our families are continuing prayer for his healing.

PREPARATIONS FOR TRANSPLANT, HICKMAN CATHETER, FINAL BONE MARROW BIOPSY, CHEMOTHERAPY, AND RADIATION

Argerine, George, and the grands, Wade,
Blakely, and Kelci in the swing

Blessed is the one who perseveres under trial because,
having stood the test, that person will receive the
crown of life that the LORD has promised.
—James 1:12

Tuesday, February 17, 1998, would be the first of many days of concern for Lisa and I; however, Wade continued to be brave and upbeat. He would say, "Mom, Dad, just think, I won't be getting needle-stuck all the time after today." The Hickman replaced the need for most needles, which saved him much discomfort, but the surgical insertion of the Hickman and his last biopsy required general anesthesia of two or more hours. The last bone marrow biopsy indicated the amount of healthy cells remaining in his blood. From this the doctors determined the amount of chemotherapy and radiation needed to prepare for the transplant.

Of course we let everyone know Wade's schedule, and on this day we could feel the prayer and love covering us. He came through the procedures with no problems, other than taking several hours to recover. Thank GOD for His protection and for the prayers of family and friends.

A daily routine helped Wade know what to expect each day and what was expected of him. This also offered the comfort and security of continued expectations and behavior. Good skin care, frequent mouth care, a daily shower, and getting dressed were scheduled along with Hickman dressing changes, weigh-ins, blood draws, and vital signs. Other parts of his routine were physical therapy, playtime, and even one he learned to enjoy; school!

This will be the first of many occasions that I will thank Wade's team at Duke and recognize them for their care. Just first class, all of them.

CONDITIONING BEGINS WITH CHEMO AND RADIATION

Wade and Blakely with cousins, from left: Bud,
Marti, Andy, Bubba, Deron, Bruce, and Kip

*When you pass through the waters I will be with you; and
when you pass through the rivers they will not sweep over you.*
—Isaiah 43:2

Like a lot of folks you are probably thinking the chemo and radiation was used as it is in cancer patients, to kill cancer cells. This was not the case with Wade. He had fanconi's anemia, not cancer. In a Pediatric BMT these treatments were used to condition the patient.

The healthy cells remaining in his blood would be destroyed by the chemo, followed by the radiation totally suppressing his immune system. All of this was required so that his body would receive and not reject the gift of life from his sister, Blakely, healthy and perfectly matched bone marrow.

On Wednesday, Feb. 18, 1998, Wade started chemotherapy. Radiation was administered on Monday, Feb. 23, 1998. He received the Bone Marrow Transplant on Wednesday the 24th. The doctors warned us of him being violently ill during his conditioning; Wait until you hear about these miracles!

I often hear parents say how they are torn between children, like when at the same time their children are playing in different ball games or graduating from middle school and elementary school, etc. Imagine this; your fourteen-year-old daughter is in the Children's Wing at Duke University Hospital. She is under full anesthesia while surgeons drill into her hip, drawing out bags of bone marrow. At the same time two floors up your eleven-year-old son is in the Pediatric BMT Unit hooked up to five IV pumps. He has no healthy blood cells and no immune system.

For Lisa and me on Feb. 24, 1998, this was not an imagination, this was reality. What do you do now? YOU PRAY! You pray hard and you get everyone else you can to pray with you!

TRANSPLANT DAY,
FEB. 24, 1998
(PART ONE)

Kligman and Fleming
Attorneys at Law
1804 Bull Street
Columbia, S.C. 29201
Telephone (803) 254-4751

Melton Kligman
Pearce W. Fleming

Mailing Address:
P.O. Box 12125
Columbia, S.C. 29211-2125

To WADE:

I know you through your grand aunt, Deloris, who works for me as my Secretary / RE INU.

Deloris has spoken of you many Times about how wonderful, smart and brave you are. I know you are going through some Tough Times but I undu you are a Tough boy — So You'll come through all this OK. Keep your spirits up and we will keep saying our prayers — God Bless you

M. Kligman

Kligman and Fleming

Therefore, let us draw near to the throne of grace, so that we may receive mercy and find grace in time of need.
—Hebrews 4:16

Let us remember the miraculous! If you will recall, the doctors told us to prepare for Wade to be terribly sick for his conditioning. Not so at all during the chemo which lasted several days. Thank the LORD! After completing the chemotherapy he received radiation the next day. He was sick that night, but joy comes in the morning. He woke up for the big day feeling great.

On Feb. 24, 1998, Blakely was downstairs giving and Wade was upstairs ready to receive. Blakely had been drilled in her back hip with a tube large enough to extract several bags of bone marrow. Wade was being administered medications through his Hickman catheter. Meemaw and Lisa's sister Lynnette were there with us as we went back and forth. We had prayed together and were continuing to pray and had asked everyone else we could contact to pray. During times like these, believers need the grace of GOD ALMIGHTY, the comforting presence of the HOLY SPIRIT, and the healing power of our LORD JESUS CHRIST! Although the hospitals and staff at Duke University were among the best in the world, we could not depend on them alone.

Our precious and brave daughter Blakely had done her part. Her ordeal was over. She was in recovery and doing fine. Her gift of life-saving bone marrow for Wade was on the way upstairs.

TRANSPLANT DAY,
FEB. 24, 1998
(PART TWO)

State of South Carolina

Office of the Governor

DAVID M. BEASLEY
GOVERNOR

POST OFFICE BOX 11369
COLUMBIA 29211

March 10, 1998

Mr. Wade Altman
Room 5203
Duke University Medical Center
Durham, North Carolina 28770

Dear Wade,

I have recently learned that you are at Duke University Medical Center and I just
wanted to write a brief note to let you know that you are in my thoughts and prayers.

I read with great interest the article about the tremendous courage you have
demonstrated in your ongoing battle with Sanconie's Anemia. In the face of the kind of
hardship that most of us will never have to endure, you have proven to be a truly brave
and spirited young man. You serve as a great inspiration and joy to all who know you
and have read of your experience.

Please be assured that you remain in the thoughts and prayers of many of your fellow
South Carolinians, the Beasley family included. May God richly bless you as you
continue to make progress. Please let me know if I can ever be of help to you or your
family in any way.

Sincerely,

David M. Beasley

Governor David Beasley

Blakely on Wade's shoulder, 2001

Therefore, since Christ suffered in his body, arm yourselves also with the same attitude, because whoever suffers in the body is done with sin. As a result, they do not live the rest of their earthly lives for evil human desires, but rather for the will of God.
—1 Peter 4:1–2 (Purity and Persecution)

GOD never intends for suffering to defeat us. Rather, HIS purpose is for it to make us holy and effective witnesses for CHRIST.
—Dr. Charles Stanley

W hen people hear about any kind of transplant, most think it involves surgically removing the organ from the donor and then surgically placing it in the patient recipient. If there was a blessing in all of this for us, it was that the most invasive part of the actual transplant was performed on Blakely in order for her to donate her bone marrow. As far as Wade receiving the marrow it was painless. It was infused through his Hickman catheter. Actually the afternoon went very well as Blakely recovered completely. Doctors and nurses celebrated how healthy her marrow was, while Lynnette, Meemaw, Lisa, and I thanked the LORD for the gift of life flowing into Wade's body. Of course no big deal to our son, always the brave one! We were interrupting his video game, but we all knew how thankful he was.

Okay, it is time to share another miracle. I told you there would be many. The doctors said that while Wade was receiving the marrow there would be a foul odor in the room. Nurses said the most effective remedy for the smell was to have a bag of oranges ready to slice. Well, guess what, we forgot the oranges. It did not matter! The air in the room was not filled with an odor or a smell but with a sweet fragrance. This was the work of GOD! Imagine holding your newborn son or daughter or grandchild and that sweet precious scent filling your nostrils. That is the aroma we all experienced in Wade's room that day. I am telling you, JESUS WAS ON A MIRACLE ROLL!

The Duke staff asked us not to be anxious because it might have taken several days or even weeks to see any improvement in Wade's blood counts. The very next day with the very first blood test his platelets, red cells and white cells began to increase! Doctors, nurses, and other staff all were amazed. We thanked GOD!

I would once again like to thank the staff at Duke University Children's Hospital and those in the Pediatric Bone Marrow Transplant Unit for the love and care given to Wade, in my opinion one of the best hospitals and staff in the country, if not the world.

HOSPITAL DAYS WITH VISITORS AND MAIL, FEBRUARY AND MARCH 1998

Duke Basketball

*For You make me glad by Your deeds, LORD. I
sing for joy at what Your hands have done!*
—Psalm 92:4

The days in the hospital before and after Wade's transplant were good, other than the night of the radiation. This was the only time he was sick. His caregivers were surprised, we were not. Seeing the constant improvement in his daily blood tests we were just joyous and thankful to God for his progress. We actually looked forward to each test, confident the results would be good, never taking a step back.

Lisa and I would trade twelve-hour shifts at the hospital, having little time together. Family members and friends would make the long drive up to Durham and relieve us for a few hours, but we were always glad to get back. Of course we missed Blakely terribly as she was in Georgetown with Aunt Kay and Uncle Luckey going to school and playing softball.

We were always excited and happy for Wade when visitors would come. There were so many I would hate to leave someone out. His friend Tyler and family from Georgetown came up. A local musician visited several times to jam and sing with Wade. Players and coaches from the Duke Basketball team came into the Unit and visited the children and their families. They signed the team photo for Wade; he was thrilled. We were all comforted and encouraged to see Pastor David and Ms. Jho Coker.

Mail delivery was maybe our favorite time of the day. Along with so many phone calls of support and love, Wade received a large amount of US mail. Cards, letters, books, gifts, and so many thoughtful notes and things; these were very special. Other than getting the daily good news of our son's blood reports there was not a better hour in the day.

OUT OF THE HOSPITAL, INTO THE RV

Wade and favorite cat, quilt, and finger

Power Ranger Wade

*Now faith is confidence in what we hope for
and assurance about what we do not see.
— Hebrews 11:1*

In the photos, Wade is asleep with his favorites: index finger, cat named Thumper, and quilt made by his Nana Pearl Altman and his pose as a Power Ranger.

It is now the middle of March 1998. You will recall the doctors warned us of Wade's recovery time being months if not a year or more. He had been in the Pediatric Bone Marrow Transplant Unit at Duke University Hospital less than a month. All of his daily test results were approaching normal. We thanked GOD! Of course, he was still required to receive medications by IV in his Hickman catheter. This did not stop him from enjoying time in the Unit away from his room. He would exercise by making laps in the halls pushing his IV pole with six pumps on it. The family room was a welcome getaway also, where we would watch movies or television and play games.

Many children in the Unit were not as fortunate, their recovery time taking longer and sometimes with complications. Lisa became friends with a mother whose child was struggling and prayed with her for healing and encouragement. Wade lost his hair, but his strength was returning. His skin and complexion...like that of a healthy infant! Even the sweet smell continued around him. We were just so thankful, so thankful.

Wade wanted to personally thank all of his caregivers. He decided to play and sing for them on the day of his release. He chose the song "Arise My Love" by Newsong, some of the lyrics were: "Sin, where are your shackles? Death, where is your sting? Hell has been defeated! The grave could not hold the KING!"

The doctors, nurses, and staff who had treated Wade filled his room, out the door and in the hall. With his guitar in hand and the track playing on his boom box he sang with a strong voice on pitch and kept rhythm on the strings in tune and key. It was powerful! There was not a dry eye in the group...some even lifting their hands in praise.

DAYS OF RECOVERY
IN DURHAM, NC

Wade and I at the Lincoln Memorial

*I will say of the LORD, "HE is my refuge and
my fortress, my GOD in whom I trust."*
—*Psalm 91:2*

In the photo Wade and I are in Washington DC at the Lincoln
Memorial, December 1999.

Continuing now in March of 1998, we thanked the Lord for Wade's rapid recovery after the BMT and believed his progress would be even better in the weeks to come. The RV that was so graciously loaned by Wade's Uncle Terry Bryant and delivered and set up by his Grandfather George Blakely is in a park near the hospital. Lisa and I slept there while trading shifts at the Unit and we are now looking forward to time together with Wade and Blakely when she comes on the weekends.

Wade was required to wear a filter mask and was restricted to the RV for the first week. His Hickman Catheter remained in place if needed after he began a regimen of oral medications. We had to take him back to Duke for weekly checkups or sooner if any problems arose. Being near the hospital was a necessity, just in case.

The weather in Durham was cold! The pipes in our RV froze several times, but thankfully none burst. We used ceramic heaters that kept us snug and LP gas for cooking and hot water. The campground was clean and quiet with a gas refill area and a laundromat. The manager on site was a nice fellow. We missed our home and family and especially Blakely when she was not there, but we were comfortable and so thankful to God for Wade's recovery.

My wife, Lisa, being an excellent cook and nurse for Wade, kept us well fed and content. I am talking about fried chicken and rice and gravy, hot breakfast and coffee in the mornings. I had never been much for coffee until that cold week in Durham…it was wonderful. There was a dining booth in the kitchen area facing a mirror on the wall. Wade would sit opposite us and the mirror, singing songs and making faces. His head was bald and his face round from the steroids, but the color and touch of his skin was brand-new. He coined two phrases during those first days in the RV. When he was hungry he would say "Must have nourishment!" and when he needed the bathroom he said "Must remove waste product!"

We didn't know how long we would be there, but we knew Wade had recovered far much faster than the doctors planned, no doubt because of all the prayer and love from family and friends and most of all from the healing touch of Jesus.

GOING HOME SOON

Wade and Joey Carter

*And he came near and kissed him, and he smelled the smell
of his raiment, and blessed him, and said, See, the smell of
my son is as the smell of a field which the LORD has blessed.*
—Genesis 27:27

In the photo Wade is with his coach, local vocalist and musician
Joey Carter.

Nearing April of 1998 in Durham spring is beginning to show up. Birds are singing, pear trees and azaleas are budding, and tame squirrels are everywhere in the RV park. Missing our cats we enjoyed the little fellows as they would take food from your hand. Wade continued to improve and grow stronger while impressing his nurse during follow-up care. His homebound teacher kept him current in his courses, with plans for being ahead of schedule upon returning to Georgetown. Aunt Nette (Lynnette) came up on weekends, bringing Blakely with her. What a blessing it was to have them with us. Lynnette would stay with the children while Lisa and I enjoyed time together eating out and buying groceries. She helped soon-to-be-licensed driver Blakely by letting her practice in the campground with her convertible. We couldn't watch, while Wade thought it was cool and eagerly awaited his turn, still sporting his filter mask.

With the weather beginning to warm we were able to enjoy some tennis. When Lynnette was there Lisa and I took turns hitting balls with her on a court near the park. We met some fellow tennis enthusiasts who worked at the hospital, a male nurse I played singles with and a couple who Lisa and I engaged in mixed doubles. Wade came with us for the doubles and enjoyed being out and about. After the match we treated him to his favorite double cheeseburger from BK, prepared especially for Duke Pediatric Bone Marrow Transplant patients. They were very understanding, as were everyone in Durham we were fortunate to meet.

I had a phone line installed in the RV which we all enjoyed, not many cell phones available at that time, as I said earlier. My friend and mentor from Liberty Life, Tom Propes, called every week to check on Wade. He took time out of his busy schedule to do this for us. Always positive and with words of encouragement, I was grateful for him then and today.

That baseball season the Durham Bulls were the Triple-A affiliate of the Tampa Bay Rays. The weekend before opening day the Rays came to town for a series with the Bulls. Wayne and Jaime from work came up and treated me to the Saturday afternoon game. We were able to see Wade Boggs and Fred McGriff play. It was a good day.

Of course I could not miss Blakely's first game as a Georgetown Bulldog. I drove down for the game then turned around and drove back. She played a good game, so well in fact they moved her to the varsity team even though she was in middle school. Yes! She was that good!

In the first week of April we got the news we had been waiting to hear: we could go home! Our final day at Duke University Hospital was to remove the Hickman catheter. One last anesthesia and one last surgery, we had been through so much, but GOD was with us. Wade woke up smiling from ear to ear, ready to go home, see his friends, his room, play his music and his video games, and we were ready to take him.

Once more, we would like to thank all of the healthcare professionals in the Pediatric Bone Marrow Transplant Unit of Duke University Hospital for their treatment of Wade. They were some of the best in the world, no doubt in my mind.

We are so thankful for friends, church, and family who prayed for and supported us during our time away. For Wade's healing touch, we thank GOD THE FATHER, GOD THE SON, and GOD THE HOLY SPIRIT, and HIS unfailing love, mercy and grace.

WHITE KNUCKLES ON
THE STEERING WHEEL

Baby Wade and Cousin Marti

In all this you greatly rejoice, though now for a little while you may have had to suffer grief in all kinds of trials. These have come so that the proven genuineness of your faith—of greater worth than gold, which perishes even though refined by fire—may result in praise, glory, and honor when JESUS CHRIST is revealed.
—1 Peter 1:6–7

In the photo Wade is three months old during Christmas 1986 with Cousin Marti at Aunt Kay and Uncle Luckey's home.

The day after Blakely was born, Lisa and I were getting ready to take her home. It took both of us to get the tiny little dress on her that Meemaw had sewn. Socks and booties and bonnet also, she was a beautiful gift from GOD. Slowly and carefully we carried her down to the car and just as slowly and carefully fastened the child safety seat around her. Exhausted from the labor and birth of our first child, Lisa rested in the backseat by Blakely while I drove us to Maryville. My knuckles white from the grip on the steering wheel, I crept through Georgetown, taking the back roads to avoid traffic and any other danger. We arrived safe and sound just a few minutes later after what seemed like an eternity…but not at our house. Lisa wanted to stay at her mom and dad's for a few days to have help with the baby.

By the time Wade was born nineteen months later, we thought ourselves to be old pros at this baby birthing thing. The labor and delivery were not as difficult for our handsome boy, another wonderful gift from GOD. The only drama in the room was the urine stream that pelted the nurse. She said, "Yes, he is all boy!" I guess he held it until he came out. The next morning we carried him out like a sack of potatoes and I drove us home, this time with one hand on the wheel…to our house!

Back to the first week in April 1998. Wade, Lisa, and I left Duke University headed home to Georgetown. With it being a weekday Blakely was home and in school but waiting anxiously for our return, as were family and friends. Leaving the area was a little bittersweet. We had met many new friends and I knew we would probably never see them again. Wade was happy to begin the transition to a normal life and we were so very thankful as well.

On the Durham Parkway leading out of town and on Interstate 40 traffic was not heavy, it was early afternoon. Merging on to I-95 south however was a different story. Vehicles were near bumper to bumper at speeds of 80 mph and more. Here I go white knuckling on the steering wheel again! Lisa and Wade rested comfortably in the car, but until I got us off the Interstate at South of the Border I could not relax. The thought in my mind was this: how terrible it would be, how devastating if after all we had been through in the last two years we would be in a horrible accident while finally going home. I now know of these mental pictures being only a trick of the devil! The huge sombreros were a welcome sight indeed.

Wade asking "Are we there yet?" countless times was not annoying on this trip at all. Even though I had been in Georgetown for Blakely's game the week before, this arrival was different. No one had to go back! Upon entering the city limits the Welcome Home signs greeted us. Just joy unspeakable! As we turned the corner and had the first glimpse of our home and those waiting to see us: thankful, humble, not enough words to describe our emotions.

We had detailed instructions to follow for continuing Wade's care at home. For the next six months Lisa and I must monitor him closely, but hey—we are home, thank GOD.

GUARDING AGAINST ANY AND ALL INFECTIONS

Siblings day—Wade and Blakely, 2001

After the Sabbath, at dawn on the first day of the week, Mary Magdalene and the other Mary went to look at the tomb. There was a violent earthquake, for an angel of the LORD came down from heaven and going to the tomb, rolled back the stone and sat on it... The angel said to the women, "Do not be afraid, for I know you are looking for JESUS, who was crucified. HE is not here. HE has risen, just as HE said!"
—Matthew 28:1–2, 5–6

W ade and Blakely are in the photo on Siblings Day 2001.

Grateful to be home with friends, church, and family, but we were not out of the woods yet, so to speak. While continuing to seek GOD and pray for Wade's complete recovery, everyone had to help us protect him from any and all infections. We had to encourage him to exercise daily, gradually increasing his level of activity to stimulate blood circulation and strengthen his heart and lungs. This was not easy, as he enjoyed his music and video games so much. The thing that he loved outdoors, skateboarding, we could not let him do because of the injury danger. Wade was not confined indoors, but the mask was still important for him to wear at least six months after transplant. It was needed around visitors in our home, near any person who was sick or in any crowded place. Having the mask on outside in an open area, with family members at home or in the car was not required.

Hand-washing in the home was vital in preventing infection, especially before cooking, eating, and after going to the bathroom. Changing hand towels frequently was a must along with using commercial soap. Hand sanitizer was not readily available then as it is today. Also critical for fighting infection was good personal hygiene. Now this for Wade was not a problem! He did not like to be dirty or have on dirty clothes. Some days he would shower three times! He loved his cats and had fun playing and sleeping with them. This was okay, but cleaning a litter box was not, also no problem for him. He could not take aspirin because of the interference in blood platelet function.

We all loved living near the water, and as I mentioned earlier, Wade, Blakely, and Kelci grew up going to Pawleys Island and any available pool. They all swam like fish, and this was great post-transplant exercise. However, any pond or pool not spring-fed or chlorinated had to be avoided, stagnant water being infectious. Too much sun exposure was not good for Wade, but here again was not a problem. Lisa always made sure the children were covered head to toe in sunscreen, a practice she continues today.

A feeling of gritty eyes was a condition he began to develop that summer. Lacri-Lube vials were prescribed and needed to be close by for this discomfort. In addition to these eye drops we had to make absolutely sure Wade took all of his medications daily as scheduled. This was crucial. Also his follow-up appointments and lab draws, which—thankfully—we could have done in Georgetown, were not to be missed. Monitoring his condition during the next few months at that time was very important as well.

Resurrection Sunday or Easter Sunday, 1998, was our first service back at Maryville Church. Long enough for him to sing "When HE was on the cross, I was on HIS mind," I ushered Wade in the side door. He took his mask off, sang his heart out, and brought the SPIRIT down. Although he had to leave after his song, it was a wonderful homecoming for all.

With GOD's help and healing touch, Wade continued his recovery through that summer and was able to start the 1998–1999 school term on schedule. Praise the LORD!

GEORGETOWN COUNTY
PROJECT BEACH

Wade in Project BEACH

THE SCHOOL DISTRICT
of
GEORGETOWN COUNTY
SOUTH CAROLINA

presents the

Project BEACH Singers
Olivia Powell Huggins, Director
Ruth Reames and Christopher Carter, Accompanists

In Concert
Organization of American Kodály
Educators National Conference

April 30, 2000
Seattle, Washington

Seattle Concert

The Director

Olivia Powell Huggins has been the director of the Project BEACH Singers since the program's inception in 1990. She is a native of Greenwood, SC, and has degrees from Lander University and the University of South Carolina. Presently, she is the music specialist at McDonald Elementary School where she was Teacher of the Year in 1993. Serving as a church musician since age thirteen, she is the Director of Music/Organist at Georgetown Presbyterian Church. As a member of the Swamp Fox Players, she was the music director and appeared as a *Narrator* in *Joseph and the Amazing Technicolor Dreamcoat* last spring. An experienced coordinator of the arts curriculum projects, she serves on the South Carolina Arts in the Basic Curriculum Steering Committee.

The Project BEACH Singers

The Project BEACH Singers represent all attendance areas of the School District of Georgetown County and have been performing since 1990. All participants attend a three-week summer program and additional Monday afternoon classes as part of the district's Project BEACH Artistic Program which serves over 125 middle and high school music, art, and drama students. The singers captivate their audiences with a dynamic choral sound presenting choral music from various world cultures and style periods. They have represented their district at Piccolo Spoleto, Francis Marion University's Arts Alive, and at South Carolina Music Educators Association and South Carolina School Boards Association conferences. In December of 1998, they were selected to perform in the East Room of the White House and in the National Park Service's Pageant of Peace. For the past two years, thousands of grand strand television viewers have enjoyed the Time Warner broadcasts of their holiday concerts. Spring 2000 performances will include performances in the Pawleys Island Festival of Music and Art's Youth Musicfest, Piccolo Spoleto, and participation in a Charleston Southern University choral seminar.

The Curriculum

Believing that singing is the basis of all musical development, the students' recreation of choral music enables them to develop the skills essential to hearing music, conceptualizing music, and perceiving musically. Solfege singing has been the core of the choral curriculum since Victor Varner, who has studied at the Kodály Institute at Capital University, joined the summer staff in 1995. The continued integration of solfege techniques into all choral rehearsals has proven an invaluable tool in directing students from diverse musical backgrounds. Summer studies also include vocal and instrumental master classes, exploration of ethnic instruments, creative movement, and folk dancing.

PROJECT BEACH SINGERS

Raffette Alston
Wade Altman
Caroline Balthis
Christopher Barnes
Brandi Barnett
Branten Blair
Vanceto Blyden
Shaquana Brown
Adam Campbell
Christopher Carter
Chela Carter
Timothy Chandler
Elizabeth Choate
Thyeesha Coleman

Meggan Cooper
Carmen Cribb
Diana Dailey
Jonathan Doerr
K. C. Forbes
Jimmy Geiger
Meagan Graham
Maurice Greene
Monique Grissom
Heather Heistand
Amanda Hoerner
Andrea Horath
Tripp Jones

Mary Catherine Kennedy
Lauren Kiser
Joan Aida Knowlin
Lauren Lowrey
Justin Mears
Akeem Miller
Nakeya Nelson
Nicole Paschal
Lauren Poston
Elizabeth Powell
Mark Richard
Harold Smith
Karen Taylor
Blake Wilson

Chuck Gadsden, Ph.D.
Superintendent

Sylvia E. Guthrie, Ed.D.
Assistant Superintendent for Instruction

Margaret P. Miller, Coordinator
Programs for the Gifted

Ashlie D. Edmiston
Administrative Secretary

Kristi Weir
Choreographer

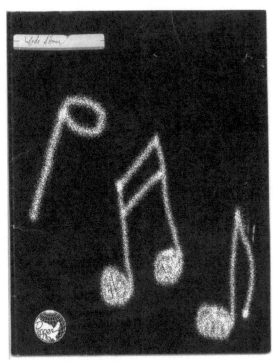

Project Folder

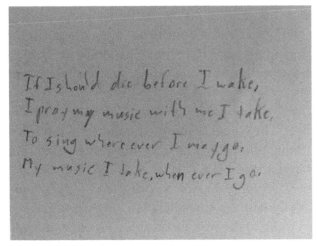

Wade's Nighttime Prayer

Wade and Woodie after concert

*My son, do not forget my teaching, but
keep my commands in your heart.*
—Proverbs 3:1

In the photos Wade is in his concert suit, the Seattle WA concert, his folder and prayer and then with me after a local concert. Inside his folder he had written this prayer; "If I should die before I wake, I pray my music with me I take, to sing wherever I may go, my music I take whenever I go."

We thank GOD for the healing in Wade's life as he continues to grow stronger. The school term of 1998 and 1999 was seventh grade and even though he had to miss so much of his sixth grade studies there was not a problem. The efforts of his homebound teachers while we were in Durham, Ms. Headly, Ms. Gockerman, and Ms. Marshall, along with his determination, all paid off. His mask was becoming a thing of the past and his hair was growing back curly!

A wonderful musician and vocalist, a masterful teacher and mentor, Project BEACH Director Olivia Powell Huggins had a profound influence on gifted and talented students in Georgetown County. This great group and Wade's coach, local artist Joey Carter, and also Tommy and Kim Gordon, our music ministers at Maryville Church, played a huge part in his recovery. He enjoyed so much the one-on-one sessions with Joey. Tommy and Kim worked with him in praise and worship, eventually promoting him into the team. Lisa and I were so very proud of our son as he continued to improve his singing and musicality.

Soon, Wade joined the Screven Baptist youth group where he made many new friends. He jumped right in to the music program where he became the drummer in their youth band. Ashley, Pat, Greg, and Phillip were several years older but they welcomed him in their music. Phillip was also the youth pastor. Along with leading praise and worship for the youth at Screven they were fortunate to play at several youth services in the area. Practicing and playing with the band meant late nights for Wade and some may have said for a thirteen-year-old in his condition it might have been too much for him. But, hey, what could we do? He was having a blast!

Project BEACH concerts were many, locally and across the country. There was always a Christmas concert at First Baptist Church which improved every year. Lisa and I were able to travel with the group to Washington, DC, in December 1999. They sang on the White House lawn for the Christmas tree lighting and at Union Train Station. The next year Lisa traveled with Wade and the Project to Seattle, WA. In early 2001, he was alone with the singers for their San Diego, CA, concerts.

Following our children around during these years were some of the best times for our family. Our All-Star softball player Blakely was on the field most of the year with the Georgetown Bulldogs and Carolina Breakers. When we were not at the ball fields with Blakely we were in concert halls or churches with Wade. You talking about a thankful and proud Mom and Dad, yes we were!

NAVAL JUNIOR RESERVE
OFFICERS TRAINING CORPS

Wade and Rachel at Navy Ball

Wade's decorations

Wade in uniform by the flag

And let endurance have its perfect result, so that you may be perfect and complete, lacking in nothing.
—James 1:4

In the photographs, Rachel and Wade are at the Navy Ball. His ribbons, medals, and beret. He is in uniform with the flag.

Wade graduated middle school with honors and began the 2000–2001 term as a freshman at Georgetown High School. He continued to excel in his studies and joined the NJROTC unit. Together with Project BEACH this program very much helped him recover physically and mentally following his bone marrow transplant. Involvement in these groups and the youth band at Screven Baptist helped him to become a very busy young man, and we thanked GOD every day. Remember what the providers at Duke predicted, that at this time we could have still been in Durham with our son, recovering. Prayers were answered!

Wade loved and respected his Captain and Master Chief. They were tough but fair and showed him no partiality due to his illness, which was the way he wanted it. Our son was fortunate enough to earn several ribbons and medals during his freshman year. He medaled twice in sharpshooting and was awarded ribbons in the following nine categories: Aptitude, Naval Science 1, Exemplary Conduct, Academics, Exemplary Personal Appearance, Participation, Unit Service, Community Service, and Rifle Team. He learned about patriotism, love for his country, and respect for the flag and the Armed Forces of the United States. His participation in the NJROTC of Georgetown High School enhanced his desire to serve in the military.

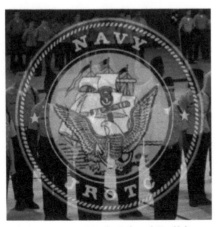

Georgetown High School Bulldogs

PROM WEEKEND 2001

Be strong and courageous. Do not be afraid or terrified because of them, for the LORD your GOD goes with you. He will never leave you or forsake you.
—Deuteronomy 31:6

The Blakelys and the grands at Maryville Church

Pictured are the Blakely's with the grands at Maryville Church; Argerine (Meemaw), Big Pop (George), Wade, Kelci and Blakely.

In the spring of 2001, Wade was three years post-transplant and doing great. So far his bone marrow infusion had been a miraculous success, an answer to many prayers of community, church, and family. Lisa and I continue to thank GOD.

Wade always had a lot of friends, most of whom were girls. However, one of his friends was Will Coggin, who was like a brother to him and Blakely and like another child to us. Blakely and Will would fight like cats and dogs with Wade taking Will's side, just burning her up! She soon learned how to avenge herself.

There were two pairs of sisters in Georgetown who through school and Project BEACH Wade became acquainted with. Every day he was on the phone with one or more of them and since they lived on opposite sides of town he was able to visit or join them at parties, ballgames, and other goings on. Blakely would soon have her revenge.

We were not yet in the age of affordable cell phones; landlines with several extensions in the home were the normal. When Wade was on a phone with one or more of his friends who were girls Blakely would sneak and listen in on another extension. After a few minutes of this she was not able to suppress her laughter, giving away her position. Wade would scream, "BLAKELY!" while whatever was in his reach would be in the air flying in her direction as he was chasing her out of the house into the yard and down the street!

I can remember Wade at the dinner table moaning his girlfriend's name over and over, "Rachel, Rachel, Rachel." Yes, he was smitten. She was his date to the Navy Ball as you read earlier. Unfortunately, soon after he and Rachel starred together in the drama class play she would no longer be able to see or talk to Wade. At this time in his life, after all he had been through this was absolutely the worst thing that could happen. He was crushed, devastated, cried for days. You are probably thinking he was only fourteen, it was just puppy love. For our son to have survived the bone marrow transplant and then to face this decision...it was a mountain for him to climb.

Only a few weeks later it was prom weekend. Blakely was a sophomore that year, so Lisa and I took her out to dinner along with Wade and Will. We celebrated Will's birthday on that Friday night, April 6, 2001. His actual birth date was the following Monday, April 9. We enjoyed the evening, but Wade didn't eat much. We boxed it up and took it home. Will stayed with us that night and he and Wade devoured the leftovers the next day.

Sunday, April 8, was the second Sunday of that month in 2001. The weather was turning warm once again and flowers were blooming. I am sure it was a great service at Maryville Church and a wonderful message by our new Pastor, Tommy Cox. Pastor David Coker had recently retired. We had lunch as usual with the family at the Blakely's. Back at home that night Wade began to complain of headache and nausea. We wasted no time taking him to the ER. After a diagnosis of possibly stomach virus they let us go home with medicine and instructions. Blakely was staying with a friend. Wade felt better.

He woke us up after midnight terribly sick. I had to carry him to the car, back into the ER and put him in a wheelchair. Lisa followed the nurse with him into the treatment area while I was trying to call everyone on the payphone. It was like I could not think, I was going in circles. Before we came back to the hospital Wade was embarrassed about being so sick in the bathroom. He said, "Oh, Dad, this is disgusting." I said, "Don't you worry son, you are the bravest boy I've ever seen!"

Before daybreak, a team of doctors and nurses had gathered to treat Wade. Pastor Tommy Cox was there with a prayer group from Maryville Church. Lisa had never left his side, and when I joined them he was unconscious. The doctors were firing questions at us, desperately trying to find out what could make him so sick so quickly. They asked us to go out while they prepared him for airlifting down to MUSC. I watched as they rolled him out to the helicopter, he was intubated.

APRIL 9, 2001: ABSENT FROM THE BODY—PRESENT WITH THE LORD!

Wade at school

*And afterward, I will pour out my SPIRIT on all people.
Your sons and daughters will prophesy, your old men
will dream dreams, your young men will see visions.*
—Joel 2:28

The early morning hours of Monday, April 9, 2001, were like a blur, like a bad dream, a nightmare. Lisa and I were in the car with Meemaw and Big Pop, Wade's grandparents, racing down to MUSC. There was no conversation.

Three years almost to the day we had been back home with Wade, his bone marrow transplant so far was a complete success, surpassing all expectations.

I could see the look of despair on the faces of the doctors and nurses in the emergency room, some of them unable to hold back their tears. They were doing the best they could, the infection was ravaging his body. The only thing the rest of us could do was pray.

At a time of HIS choosing, when Wade was in the ER, in air transport to MUSC or after his arrival there, the LORD took our son home. We won't know exactly when or where until we get home ourselves, but we know beyond any shadow of any doubt that he is in glory with JESUS!

Now, please do not be upset. After reading Wade's story thus far, I am sure this is not what you wanted to learn. We truly believed he would live a full and happy life, but that was not GOD's plan. Please continue with the book and please keep an open mind. Some of the things I am about to share might be difficult to understand.

The next hours and days for Lisa, Blakely, me, and our family were horrific. If it were not for the prayer covering us and for the comforting HOLY SPIRIT we would not have been able to cope. Extended family, church, friends, and community were all grieving with us.

The McKenzie home took care of the arrangements for Wade and did a wonderful job. Lisa coordinated with them for the service at Maryville, assisted by many of the staff at our church. Hundreds lined up at his visitation and hundreds more attended his home-going celebration. Patrick McCall and the NJROTC drill team honored our son as well as Olivia Powell Huggins and the Project BEACH singers. Pastor Phillip McCart and the Screven Baptist youth band ministered along with Tommy and Kim Gordon and our Maryville music leaders. Blakely's Coach Squires and her teammates took part. Pastors

David Coker and Tommy Cox officiated. Wade's cousins Bubba and Bruce Sanders, Deron, Kip and Andy Nettles, Bud Campbell and Dusty Bryant were pallbearers. Many of his recordings were played during the service.

At Maryville Church, we are blessed to have so many talented and anointed people; preachers, singers, musicians, elders, teachers, and a precious Woman of God who ministers in the prophetic. Her name is Bonnie Charlton and in Wade's story she has a very important part.

On the Sunday after Wade's passing, Lisa and I were determined to get to church and, thankfully, we did. We could not understand why GOD would allow this and we desperately needed direction to be able to go on. After the service, Ms. Bonnie called us to the side, saying she had received a word of knowledge from the LORD concerning Wade and wanted to share it with us. She said GOD had given our son a glimpse of Glory, of Heaven, of what no man has felt in his heart, has heard with his ear, or seen with his eye. She said Wade was given a choice and he chose to be with his GOD.

The weeks, months, and years have not been easy for Lisa, Blakely, and me. We have been sustained by the grace, mercy, and love of our LORD and savior JESUS CHRIST. After the loss, Lisa and I are stronger and closer in marriage. Lisa has been able to minister to women in our church, district, and in the local Community Bible Study. I am honoring Wade by continuing music ministry at Maryville Church and am blessed to be with the Cribb's, who have been playing and singing Southern Gospel for many years.

Blakely perhaps struggled more than anyone else. She was angry for a long time, but has grown into a strong and independent young woman. A successful massage therapist, she has recently opened Sweetgrass Boutique and Day Spa in Georgetown. There are not enough words to describe how proud I am of her.

Second Samuel chapter 12 verses 22 and 23:
He answered, "While the child was still alive, I fasted and wept. I thought, who knows? The LORD may be gracious to me and let the child live. But now that he is dead, why should I go on fasting? Can I bring him back again? I will go to him, but he will not return to me."

AFTERMATH

Our family, 2001

Our family, 2018

No ear has heard, no eye has seen, and no heart has imagined what GOD has prepared for us. We will not understand the reasoning behind so many trials of this life until we see JESUS, then all will be crystal clear.

However, of this I am sure: without the tragedy that Lisa and I had to face, our marriage would not have survived. Very few people know that shortly after the time of Wade's diagnosis, we began a very difficult time in our married life, with many years of heartbreak and rejection. This had nothing to do with our son's illness or from any fault of Lisa. No, this burden fell squarely on my shoulders. Let me be clear, not only was she battling for Wade's life, she was living with the consequences of my sin. We have seen many miracles in Wade's story, but one of the greatest is that not only did our marriage endure, I believe Lisa and I are closer now than we have ever been! All Glory to GOD!

In many chapters of our son's story you have read about the bravery and courage not only of Wade, but also of his sister Blakely. Without the healthy bone marrow she so willingly gave, her brother's near future was uncertain. For Blakely, the years after losing him were a dark time. Like all of us she had doubts and questions, but Lisa and I and her family and friends were there for her. Of most importance the LORD JESUS CHRIST was by her side, shielding and protecting her. Blakely has come to realize these things in her life and she knows the favor of GOD. She is now the mother of a precious boy, Mason Wade Altman, "Mase," our grandson. What a blessing! What a wonderful gift from GOD he is!

Ephesians 3:20–21: "Now to him who is able to do all we ask or imagine, according to his power that is at work within us, to him be the glory in the church and in CHRIST JESUS throughout all generations, forever and ever! Amen."

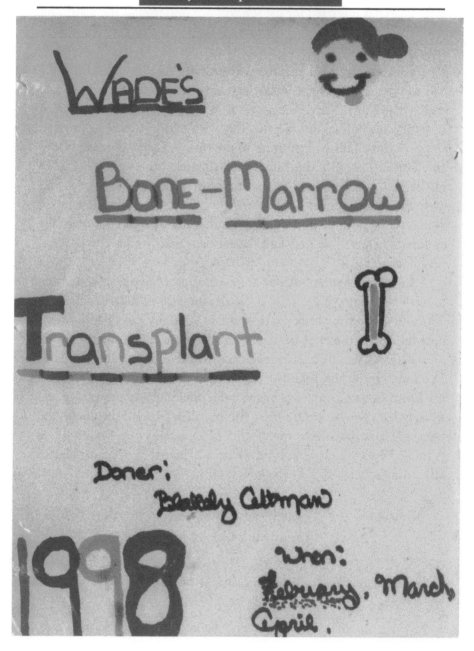

It's hard saying by to friends
and family.
Expecially for Wade who
has never been away
from home more than a
week and now 3 months

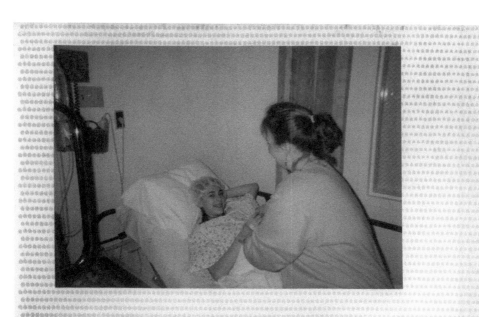

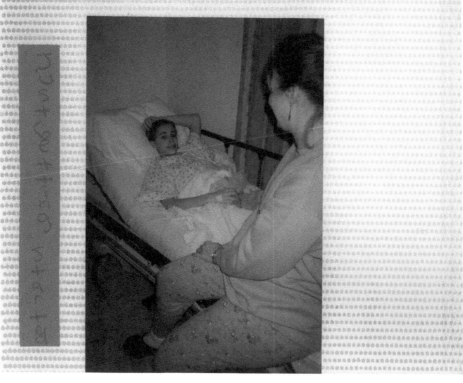

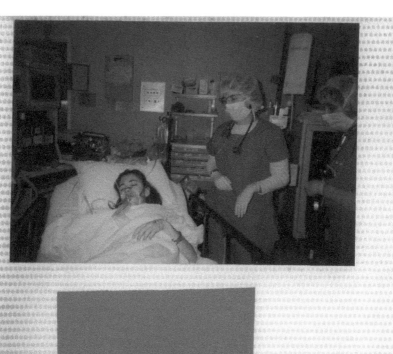

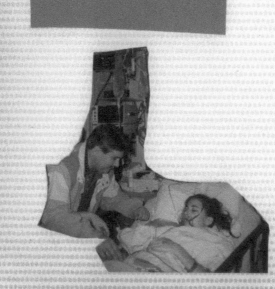

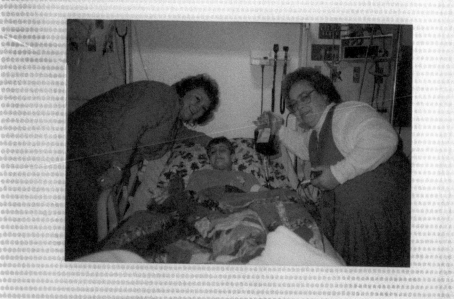

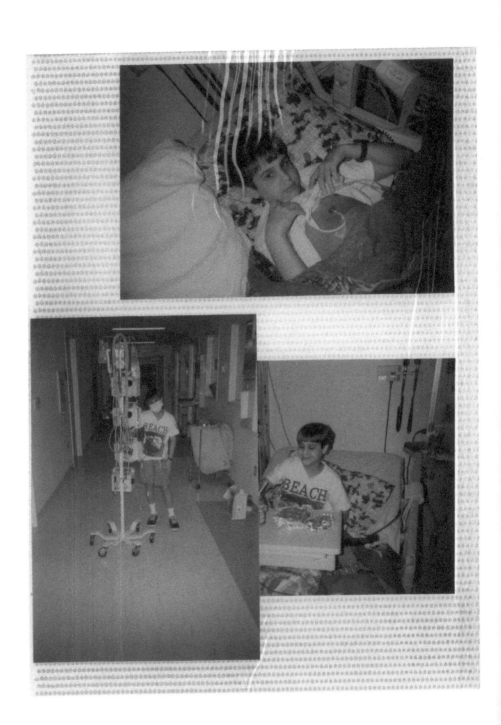

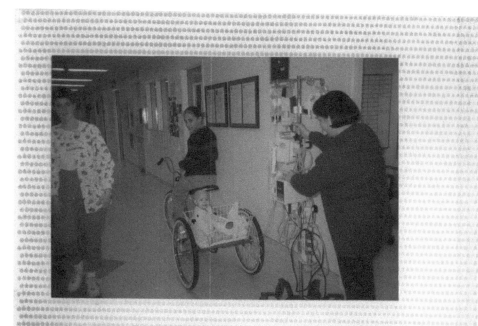

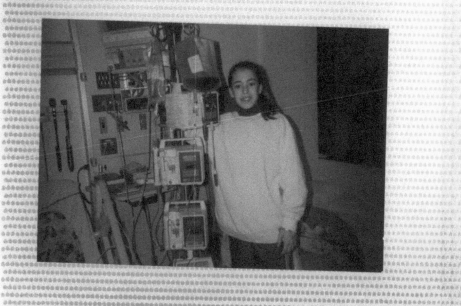

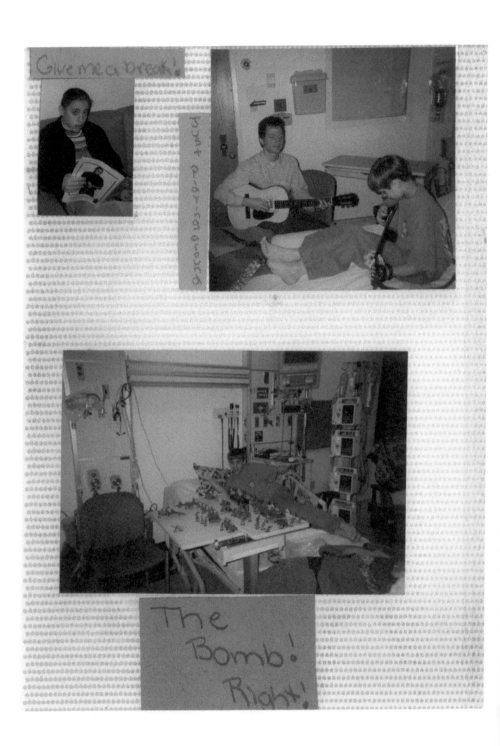

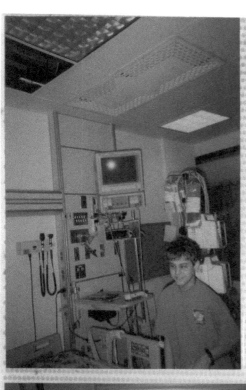

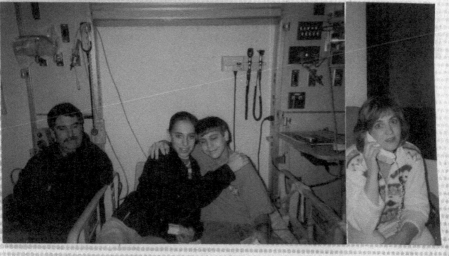

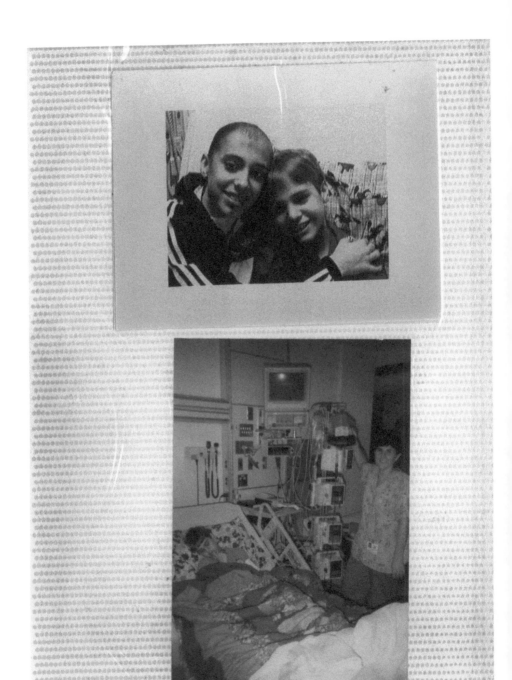

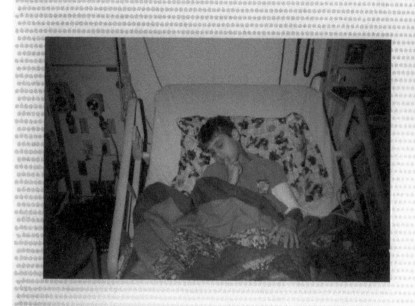

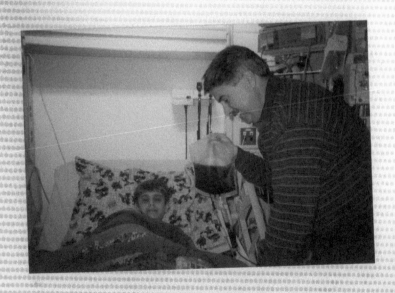

2-10-97
4:45 p.m.

BLAKELY,

I MISS you!!

GUESS WHAT HAPPENED THIS
MORNING! THE WATER IN THE
CAMPER WAS FROZEN!

DAAGGUMMIT!!

SHHHHHH!!

I JUST HAD A SHOWER AND
SHAVE AND YOUR MOTHER JUST
WASHED, NO, HAS NOT WASHED HER
HAIR YET!

AIN'T NO SENSE IN THAT!

⟶

SERIOUSLY, WE'RE BLESSED TO HAVE THE CAMPER AND THE R.V. PARK IS NICE. WE'VE HAD TWO GOOD DAYS.

WE LOOK FORWARD TO SEEING YOU THURSDAY.

THANKS AGAIN FOR TAKING CARE OF THE CATS AND FISH. PET THE CATS AND TALK TO THEM FOR ME.

I LOVE YOU!

DADDY

P.S.— TELL MEE MAW AND AUNT NETTE WE'LL BE GLAD TO SEE THEM TOO!

Dearest Blakely   2-10-98

    Hey! It's a BEAUTIFUL day here.
Daddy & I just walked around the campground & took the trash. We thank God
for this place to stay - it is really
a blessing. Wade is playing the
Play Station. We found LOTS of places
to shop today so hopefully we
can take a break sometimes and shop.
If Daddy and I cannot go with you,
maybe MeeMaw can. We are having
Hamburger Helper for supper tonight -
Yummy ☺. We ate at the mall
food court today. Wade had Chinese food. Daddy & I had steak
Kabobs. We're trying to stay away
from that GROSS Hosp. Cafeteria.

Hey Blakely!
As you know, My counts are now 57.
I'm having a pretty good time, but really miss
you. Can't wait to see ya'!

Love,
Wade

Hope you get to have softball ②
practice tomorrow — Don't for get to
bring your gloves + balls — it's boring
around here — so we will have
time to play.

We miss you very much.
Wish you were here to
make us laugh.

We love you I love
you — God loves you ☺

Hugs + kisses

Love + prayers,
Mom

See
ya
Soon

Keep
cool
Kiddo

HA-HA
HA-HA

P.S.
Wade's soon
will have Email
so find out your
friends #.

Blakely, Lisa, and Mason Wade

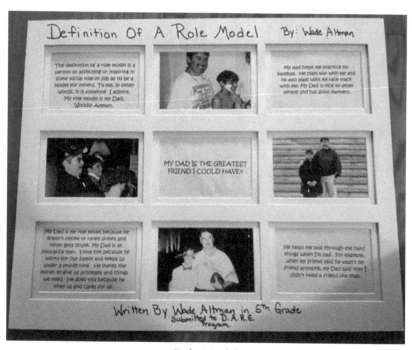

Role Model

Lisa and Blakely

Mason Wade and Whitman

Georgetown High School
P.O. Box 1778   2500 Anthuan Maybank Drive   Georgetown, SC 29442-1778
Telephone: (843) 546-8516

14 May 2012

Mr. and Mrs. Woody Altman
913 Lakeside Drive
Georgetown, SC 29440

Mr. and Mrs. Altman,

Thank you so much for your continued support to the Georgetown High School Naval Junior ROTC Unit annual Awards Ceremony on Thursday, the 10th of May. The ceremony was a success and we were delighted you were able to come and present the Wade Altman Courage Award this year to Cadet Katie Bogan, an excellent graduating Cadet.

Mr. Altman, Katie was very touched that you personally presented this award. It is especially nice the presentation was made by you instead of the principal or naval science instructor who are well known to the cadets. It certainly enhances the meaning of the medal to everyone when someone outside the school takes the time to come to our ceremony.

We are delighted that you remain interested in supporting the Naval Junior ROTC Program at Georgetown High School. Please know that the Wade Altman Courage Medal helps play a significant role in reinforcing the values we try to instill in the cadets. We look forward to having you present a medal to a deserving candidate at next year's ceremony in early May, probably the 9th. We will contact you in the spring with more details.

Sincerely,

C.L. (Dean) Brown
CAPT USN (Ret)
GHS NJROTC SNSI

Letter from Captain Dean Brown

In memory of Sherman Standridge; a wonderful musician and singer, an anointed preacher and evangelist, our friend and partner in ministry—a true Man of God. Our brother, we miss you, but one day we will sing and play together again.

Sherman Standridge

ABOUT THE AUTHOR

Thank you for considering *Wade's Story*. The author is Martin L. Altman III, "Woodie", a lifetime resident of the Georgetown, SC, area. His wife of thirty-seven years is Lisa Blakely Altman, also a lifetime resident of Georgetown.

Lisa and Woodie have been blessed with two children, Blakely Renee Altman and Wade Hampton Altman, and one grandson, Mason Wade Altman.

After graduating Winyah High School in 1972, Woodie continued working in supermarket retail. In 1987, he made a career change to life and health insurance as an agent and manager.

Lisa also graduated Winyah in 1982. After staying home with Blakely and Wade before they started school, she earned a nursing degree from Horry-Georgetown Technical College and has worked as a licensed practical nurse since 1992.

Woodie and Lisa were blessed to grow up in Christian families with direction and love. Lisa's parents were charter members of Maryville Pentecostal Holiness Church while Woodie's mom and dad helped charter Wayne Methodist Church. A membership change was required, however, because initially Lisa and Woodie could only see each other at church! He has been at Maryville since then.

Lisa has served in women's ministries for many years and also in Community Bible Study. Woodie served as a deacon and is ministering in music at Maryville and with the Cribb's, who have been singing and playing Southern gospel in the area for decades.

Woodie thanks GOD for Lisa, their children, the blessings of health, and the saving grace of the LORD JESUS CHRIST.

Lightning Source UK Ltd.
Milton Keynes UK
UKHW021049210921
390904UK00007B/398